101
Plus Size Women's Clothing
Tips

LifeTips Book Series

By Lynda Moultry
Plus Size Women's Clothing Expert Guru
LifeTips

LifeTips
Move Up In Life.

LifeTips Book Series
Boston, Massachusetts

LIFETIPS PRESIDENT: Byron White

BOOK SERIES EDITOR: Melanie Nayer

LifeTips.com, Inc.
101 Book Series
One First Avenue
Building 34, Suite 200
Charlestown, MA 02129
(617) 886-9001

http://www.LifeTips.com

International Standard Book No. 978-1-60275-001-2

Table of Contents

A Note from the Editor

Did you know that Marilyn Monroe's dress size was a 12? Her bust size was a 36D, and depending on which tailor you ask, she fluctuated between a size 8 and a size 10 pant. By Hollywood's standards, Marilyn Monroe was perfect...back then. By today's standards, the legendary starlet would be forced to lose weight and show off more bones, and less curves. Thank goodness not everyone in the fashion industry has succumbed to Hollywood standards.

Today's women are curvier, sexier, bustier and better in all the right places, and designers are taking note. Designers are realizing that not all women are a size 2 but everyone deserves to look good no matter what their shape or size. From the runway to the driveway, women are catwalking their way to better fitting-clothes, and better lifestyles.

This tip book was created with one thing in mind: if you look good, you feel good! Lynda Moultry took her years of fashion industry experience and created 101 tips for you - the full-figured fabulous woman - to reenergize your wardrobe and your lifestyle.

So ladies, stay P.H.A.T.... and flaunt every curve to its fullest.

Melanie Nayer, Editor
LifeTips

A Note from the Author

The plus-size fashion topic is so hugely important, both to me and to millions of women out there. For so long, there has been little in the way of fashion advice and education for full-figured women. Additionally, fun and sexy trends were not made for women of size, relegating us to clothing that was more frumpy, and less fashionable.

But look out, ladies! There is a revolution afoot and the fashion industry has taken note. We are demanding designers offer us fashion options that are fresh and edgy and make the most of our fabulous curves. Because of that, many boutiques now cater to plus-sizes, some even exclusively. The clothing is stylish, the staffs are usually knowledgeable about what works on our figures (and are often plus-sized as well) and the options are unlimited.

This book is designed with that attitude in mind. It is time to throw out that old wardrobe and get ready to shake things up! We're talking about colorful tunics, sexy wrap dresses, sophisticated denim, bright accessories, the hottest footwear and a revamped outlook on why being a plus-sized woman means you have the ability to be stylish, bold and fabulous! Most mainstream trends now translate to larger sizes and we are learning that it is important not to hide what we have, but to flaunt it baby!

Take the tips in this book and apply them to your wardrobe - your personal style - your life. Build up the confidence to know that no matter what, you are a beautiful, amazing, full-figured woman. Once you really believe that, it will show from the inside out and you will know how to work those curves to look spectacular in just about anything!

Lynda Moultry,
LifeTips Expert Guru

1| Midsection Definition Key For Apple Shapes

Plus-size women with an "apple" shape are characterized by a shapely figure that is thick throughout the middle. Apple shapes usually have ample busts, thick midsections and slimmer hips and legs.

Choose clothing for definition around the middle portion of the body. These body types look best in A-line styles. It is best for "apple" women to create looks that have a slimming effect at the waist, such wearing a funky belt with tunics and button down shirts and tailored jackets that hit just below the waistline.

2| V-Necks A "Do" For Apples

Chunky clothing, such as bulky sweaters, tops that swim around your figure and long, thick jackets are a no-no for apple shapes. These styles only makes you look bigger and accentuate your full figure.

Instead, gravitate, towards v-neck shapes in your tops. V-necks work for just about any body type because they elongate your body and have a natural slimming effect. Choose a v-neck top in a material that skims your body's silhouette instead of a clingy fabric or one that is too loose.

3| Tankinis For Tanning

Similar to pear shapes, apples should invest in the right swimsuit style to best flatter curves. Purchase a tankini for summer — a good option for apple-shaped women. One-piece suits can make you look larger than you are. A tankini offers coverage and adds shape to your figure.

Color is not as much of a consideration for your body type as style. Opt for good coverage, with a tankini top that ends right around your hips. If you have thick legs and thighs, a skirted design might be right for you. There are a lot of fun colors and patterns, and you have many options. The only pattern to avoid is horizontal stripes. Of course, darker colors do minimize your overall silhouette.

Have fun with your summer swimsuit style and pay close attention to the fit of your suit to avoid odd bumps or bulges.

4| Cotton, A-Line Dresses Look Best On Apple Shapes

A-line and empire dresses work well with apple shaped bodies. They hide all of your flaws and still manage to show off the good curves! This style narrows at the top and flares toward the bottom, which is why it is flattering for apple figures. Like an empire dress, it disguises your tummy and slims your overall silhouette. Choose fabrics that have a little stretch so it is forgiving to your size. Constricting fabrics might fit, but in a way that shows off your body in an unflattering light. Cotton is the best fabric for plus-sizes because it falls along the body's contours with being restrictive, so when choosing dresses, this should be your first choice in fabric.

5| Look For Bootcut Jeans

Bootcut jeans add balance to your overall look. Jeans that taper at the bottom unevenly contrast with the fullness of your midsection. A pair of bootcut jeans that fall below your ankle creates a slimming effect and creates the illusion of a clean line from the waist down. Apples should also look for jeans with a little stretch in order to bring the tummy in a little and really emphasize other curves, including the hips and backside.

6| Stay Away From Tight Trousers

Apple shapes should stay away from trousers that are extremely tailored or have a tight fit. The more well-defined a pair of pants is around your midsection, the more unwanted attention will go to that area.

Instead, focus on dark colored trousers that create a clean, straight line from hip to ankle. They should fit loosely (which is not the same as baggy) to give your silhouette a smoothness that will enhance your outfit.

7| The Truth About Tops

Do not wear tops that feature a lot of busy detail, like ruffles, rouching or other embellishments. This calls attention to your midsection, which is the area apple shapes usually try to minimize. Shirts should fit loosely and be solid-colored with simple designs.

Anything that clings to your stomach is a no-no; therefore, shirts with a lot of Lycra are out! You want fabrics that will fall nicely over the curves of your midsection, not make any problem areas stand out.

Apple shapes look good in ribbed fabrics, wrap tops and v-necks — all of which elongate the upper part of the body, creating a slimming effect. Great accessories contribute to a stylish look, helping to pull it all together.

8| Apples Should Go Monochromatic

A monochromatic color scheme really works well for an apple body shape. Wearing the same colors on the top and bottom creates a clean, straight line that lengthens and slims the overall silhouette of the body. The best way to be expressive with this look is to mix up the fabrics.

Try a combo of cotton and chiffon for a fun, light, flirty look. For a more serious look, try a sold-colored, tweed suit. On the other hand, you can try wearing two different variations on one color. For example, dark blue on bottom and a lighter blue on top still gives you the same straight line and let's you vary your style just a little.

9| Camis Perfect For Layering

Layering light fabrics looks good on apple figures. For example, a light cotton tank or cami looks great on an apple shape under a long-sleeved jacket or button-down top.

Layering can add some dimension to your midsection, helping to make you look shapely instead of thick. Do not layer thicker fabrics, however, because they will make you look bigger.

Camisoles work best for layering purposes because they are thin and often feature pretty embellishments, such as bead or scalloping, along the top edge of the top, spicing up whatever you wear over it.

They especially look good with structured jackets; just be sure you pay attention to the length of your top layer. Your apple shape dictates that jackets and tops should be long enough to hit your hip area to hide any hotspots.

10| The Goal for Pear Shapes Is Balance

Pear shapes aim to achieve more balance for their overall figure. To achieve this, utilize the following tips:

- Choose A-line skirts and dresses. The skirt should closely follow the contours of your curves to keep it from looking baggy and unshapely.

- Boot-cut is your best choice in jeans. The roominess below the thigh area will make your hips look smaller.

11| Pear Shape Dont's

It is important to know what looks good on your pear shape to flatter your curves. However, it is equally important to realize what kinds of clothing will work against your shape.

Do not choose pieces that will make you look wider on bottom, minimizing what is best about your fantastic curves. Here are a few additional **don'ts** for plus-size, pear-shapes:

- Don't wear loud prints or light colors on bottom

- Don't wear pants that settle above your waist

- Don't wear pants that narrow at the bottom (this will draw attention to your hips – making them stand out more than usual

- Don't wear short skirts that fit tightly around your lower half

12| Try A Pair Of Shoulder Pads

A great way to add some balance to your appearance is to perk up your clothing with padding. Be it through a padded bra or modest shoulder pads, the extra lift will help your clothing wear in a more flattering way. These days, shoulder pads are more modest with a natural-looking, rounded shape.

Slip on a pair of shoulder pads underneath your clothing and see what a different it makes in how your clothing looks on your shapely figure. The top half of your body will likely look like it better matches your lower half, which will definitely help dissolve some of your clothing dilemmas.

13| Top Looks For Pear Shapes

Top looks for pear shapes include:

- Dark, denim boot-cut jeans paired with a tailored white shirt is a fantastic, chic look. If you really want to amp it up, add a large, colorful handbag and chunky, silver jewelry. The more you enhance your outfit, the more attention people will pay to it and not your perceived flaws.

- For the office, try a square-necked shirt with an a-line skirt. The more flattering the neckline, the more likely it is to draw the eye upwards, taking the attention of your thighs!

- To make the outfit interesting and trendy, choose a bold, bright color such as red or pink on top with a dark skirt in black or navy. Do not be afraid to accessorize; no matter what shape you are, accessories always enhance your personal style.

14| Tankinis Best For Pear Shapes

Bathing suits are often a source of contention with pear shapes. It is hard to find a suit that fits well for the top and bottom portion for the body. This is even more complicated when you are also plus-sized.

Someone with this body type would look best in a tankini. Tankinis offer the coverage of a one-piece suit with the advantage of purchasing two pieces in different sizes to accommodate your body shape.

Pear shapes should look for bold color on top and darker colors on the bottom. The idea for this shape is to draw attention upward.

15| Jackets And Tops Should End At The Hips

The hips don't lie and in this instance, they are your fashion truth serum! The hipbone is the line when all tops and jackets should end on a plus-size, pear shaped figure, because this visually divides your body into two halves, minimizing the lower half.

Stay away from any jackets that are too long and do not give you that visual break, they will only make your bottom half look bigger.

Likewise, avoid cropped tops because they have the same effect. Balance is the key to plus-size, pear shape fashion and a hip-length top or jacket will make it happen!

16| Wear A Wrap Dress

A wrap dress is a perfect addition to a pear-shape's wardrobe. It drapes over the body in such a way that the lower portion is hidden, allowing the best curves to show.

Avoid busy patterns, opt for a solid-colored dress, and let your accessories be the accent. While darker colors usually look best to de-emphasize the lower half of a pear shaped body, you can go lighter with a wrap dress because of its A-line design.

Another wrap dress benefit is that it makes the most of your cleavage, no matter how big or small. It dips just low enough to make the dress sexy, without revealing too much, making the most of your overall curves. So, be sure you wear a proper-fitting bra that gives your breasts optimal support when you sport this kind of dress.

17| Accessories Belong On Top

Most accessories for pear shapes should begin and end on top. The idea behind your entire look is to draw the eye upward. So, avoid belts and embellishments on your lower half and instead focus on accessorizing the upper portion of your body.

Scarves and necklaces are a great way to decorate your neck area; funky earrings can make any outfit sing and many bracelets, either chunky or bangle, make you look flirty and fun!

Do not overload yourself with too many different pieces, because you do not want to look busy. The idea behind accessorizing up top is to create balance by add embellishments to your best body parts.

18| Footwear Can Make A Difference For Pear Shapes

The right footwear can make a big different for plus-size, pear shapes. The idea is to try to balance out the curves of your body.

Heels and knee-high boots can help do just that by creating an elongated silhouette. Not only will you likely stand taller, with better posture, but also you will look smoother and leaner.

However, comfort should always be a consideration. It is not worth it to wear uncomfortable heels all day, every day, to look leaner. Instead, try this tip for special occasions when you want to look extra good.

For every day, wear clothing that flatters you and shoes that are comfortable and keep your feet healthy.

19| Busty Types Should Invest In A Good Minimizer Bra

Busty body types look exactly how they sound: body shapes with a large bust area (which is not just your breasts, but the area around them as well). Too often, women with busty body types try (usually in vain) to hide their generous curves on top, only to end up looking bigger everywhere else.

The best tool busty figures can have in their fashion arsenal is a good, sturdy minimizing bra. This will make certain the shape and contour of your bust area is preserved, but not pushed out and on display. With a good minimizer bra, your clothes will drape over your body nicely and you can be comfortable dressing to enhance all of your beautiful curves.

20| Keep Neck Accessories Simple

Busty body types should keep neck accessories simple — too much on your neck will only make you look more top-heavy. Choose darker colors on top and try to balance your look. Indulge in belts and funky shoes to add accessories to your outfit on the lower half of your body.

Avoid pins and brooches unless you are comfortable drawing attention to the area. The same rule applies if you choose to wear loud, colorful baubles.

21| Wear A Pencil Skirt

A pencil skirt will help draw attention away from your bust area. Pencil skirts are always in style and should be a staple in every plus-size closet. They flatter curves better than any other style of skirt and come in a variety of colors and styles. A pencil skirt will show off your subtle curves on bottom, highlight your legs and create a streamlined, lean look.

For busty shapes, wear a pencil skirt with a v-neck top or a crisp, button-down top. Just be sure your top is the right size and buttons are not pulling around the bust area. If this happens, you may need to go up a size or two and then have your shirt tailored to fit your midsection.

22| V-Necks Are Best For Busty Bodies

Busty body types may find it difficult to find tops that enhance their curves without causing cleavage to bust right out of their shirt! Likewise, you do not want to be stuck wearing only dark colors.

Choose colorful tops in a v-neck style, which is slightly low-cut, but very elongating. Do not wear tops with loud prints, high necks or sleeveless cuts. This will only draw more attention to your bust area. Stay away from padding of any sort.

23| Stay Away From Baggy Tops

Avoid overly baggy tops. All too often, busty women think that hiding under baggy shirts will minimize their bust. However, it works adversely, making you look even bigger. Look for clothing with a slight shape that skim along your curves to enhance them.

Your bra is what makes the difference in how your bust looks under your clothing. If you are wearing the right bra, and you choose tops that are made to enhance plus-size curves, everything will fall right into place.

24| Large Busts Should Wear Single-Breasted Jacket

If you have a large bust and are given to wearing great suits, pay close attention to the cut of your jacket. Avoid double-breasted jackets, as they will just play up your bust even more; instead, opt for a single-breast cut and stay away from pockets around the breast area.

If need be, have the jacket altered to fit your body shape, particularly if you have a large bust and a slimmer midsection. Make sure the fabric and/or closures do not pull around the bust area. If they do, you may need to go up a size and then alter the jacket accordingly.

25| Full-length Strapless Bra Keeps Your Breasts In Place

Busty body types often have trouble finding an evening dress that fits well. You are either bulging out of the top of the gown or stuffed down in there looking flat and oddly lumpy.

The solution to this problem is a full-length, well-fitting strapless bra. Extending down to the bottom of your torso, a full-length strapless bra will hold you in place and smooth out your stomach area, making the dress fit better and look better proportioned.

Choose a neutral color and avoid a piece with a lot of extra embellishments. It should fit comfortably and just slightly snug. Too tight and you end up looking — and feeling — like a stuffed sausage the entire time you are wearing the dress. The idea isn't to look smaller or thinner — but rather, to keep your breasts in place and your overall midsection looking smoother.

26| Save Strapless For Evening

It may be difficult, but busty types should avoid strapless numbers during the day. You only want to wear strapless clothing when you are going out in the evening and want your cleavage to be on display (which can have a devastatingly sexy effect — if it's done right).

Strapless shirts and dresses give little to no support in the bust area and have minimal coverage — meaning your cleavage will be front and center. Because of the amount of skin you are showing, this is a definite no-no for the office or everyday outfits.

Do it up in a classy way for nighttime. Make sure you aren't showing too much skin. Invest in a fabulous strapless bra and make sure it doesn't peek over the top of your shirt or dress. Wearing a great jacket when you are going strapless is the best way to show a little skin and cleavage and still maintain a classy, ladylike appearance.

27| Choose Swimwear With Proper Support

Choosing the right swimwear when you are full-figured and busty is tough. It's important to have the best support possible. The best option is to purchase a suit with a built-in bra for added support. A halter style will help give you lift, but you need to be sure that you aren't bulging out of the side of the suit. A one-piece suit is best for this body type to really get the support needed to accommodate a large bust. That being said — you can still be stylish.

Choose a funky print with a v-neck style to show off a little sexy cleavage. Dark is most slimming, but let's face it, it's far more fun to get into something colorful that plays up your wonderful curvy body. Who wants to be drab all the time? It's much more fun to parlay on the beach in fun, tropical colors that showcase the fun personality you possess.

28| Simple Rules For Full-Figured Women

For women who are full-figured throughout, these simple rules apply:

- Choose outfits in monochromatic themes — this creates a slimming effect.

- Mix and match bold colors with darker separates.

- Choose fabrics that drape over your curves. Clothing with too much spandex will cinch your body too tight — and instead of creating a smooth, streamlined effect, you will end up with bulges.

29| Don't Always Look For Clothes That Slim

Ladies, ladies, ladies — don't fall too deep into the "slimming" trap. All too often, people will direct you to fashionable pieces that have a "slimming effect."

But who says we want to hide our curves? Being full-figured and curvy with a fabulous, womanly shape is wonderful you should flaunt it!

Instead of looking for clothing that makes you look slimmer, look for pieces that really make the most of your curves in the most flattering light. You want to look smooth and streamlined, which doesn't always equal slim.

Looking this good — and voluptuous — can only give you most confidence and increase your overall stylish appeal!

30| Full-Figured Actress Sets New Standards in Plus-Size Fashion

Most plus-sizes can really take a page from actress Mo'Nique's book on how to be full-figured and work it! The comedienne is coming out with her own line of clothing aimed at plus-sized women! *Fat Gurl* promises to be stylish and fun and help you to gain a sense of confidence in your personal style. She is also the brainchild of the Oxygen Network's "F.A.T. Chance" (which stands for Fabulous and Thick), a reality beauty pageant.

Mo'Nique constantly amazes with her style. From a short, swingy blue dress at 2004 BET Awards (in which she did Beyonce's "Crazy In Love" dance better than Beyonce herself) to her beautiful, white, strapless gown on the red carpet of the same event, she is the epitome of a super stylish, plus-sized woman.

Mo'Nique consistently talks about being a full-figured woman in an industry and society that tries to make it difficult to feel good about yourself inside and out. As this daring fashionista continues to make fashion waves and break down preconceived ideas of what a full-figured woman should look like, Mo'Nique will no doubt continue to shine —- on the red carpet and beyond.

31| Don't Feel Pressured To Wear Heels

There are so many fabulous flat shoe styles available, that you can go flat and still be fashionable.

Remember, your flat shoes need to go with your outfit. If you are dressing for work, choose a pair of flats that are professional — meaning no flip-flop sandals or torn soles. Choose solid colors and don't go overboard on embellishments, particularly if you work in a conservative office environment.

For play, however, the sky's the limit. There are an array of colors, designs and styles in flats these days. From ballerina-styles to colorful, rhinestone encrusted sandals, you can dazzle in flats just as well as you can in heels.

Don't feel pressured to walk around in heels when you can look just as fabulous —and feel even more comfortable — in a pair of flats.

32| Plus-Size Lingerie Options

We all want to feel sexy from time to time and lingerie is the perfect way to do that. There have been major strides in lingerie options for fuller figures and the choices are endless. Choose pieces that flatter your particular body type.

Long, flowing, thin-strapped, silk gowns are usually very flattering to plus-sizes. Choose styles with lacy embellishments on top and a deep v-neck for optimal cleavage. Short versions of this style look great on fuller figures as well.

Cute, silk short sets are another lingerie option for plus-sizes. Look for soft, pretty colors and again, shirts that really show off your cleavage.

Don't be afraid to accessorize your lingerie with beautiful jewelry and fancy bedroom shoes!

33| Check Out A Retro Denim Jacket

Jackets are tricky for fuller-figures and the right cut and style is everything. However, for casual, every day, consider a retro-style, denim jacket. They can be a fabulous way to jazz up your look just a little.

Stay away from light washes, they just make you look wider. Instead, choose a dark-wash style that falls to your hips. Make sure you choose the right style — you should be able to button the jacket. You might consider alterations if you need to buy a larger size to accommodate a larger bust or midsection.

Denim jackets go with everything — from matching jeans to a flowery, funky dress. Have fun experimenting and remember the right fit sets the tone for the rest of the outfit.

34| The Rules Of Translating Trends

Be aware of what trends translate well to plus-sizes and which ones do not. There is nothing worse than trying to keep up with the latest trends as a plus-size woman and then ending up with an unflattering style, feeling downright uncomfortable. Here are some things to keep in mind when translating trends:

- Dresses with a straight style are a don't for plus-sizes. Wrap, empire or A-line is best.

- Skinny jeans and pants only work on plus-sizes when they don't taper at the bottom, maintain a straight line from waist to ankle and are worn with long, tunic-style tops.

- Stay away from belly-baring tops. You can love your curves and flaunt them, but you still need to be classy and realistic about the most flattering way to show off your full-figured body. Layer belly-baring tops with longer tanks underneath instead.

35| Stay Far Away From Pants With Stirrups

Here is a rule of fashion to follow no matter what the situation:

Ladies, no matter what you do, never, ever, ever, EVER wear pants with stirrups around the ankles. Far too many plus-sized women get into the habit of wearing these kinds of pants — and believe me, they do not look good. Ever. With anything.

If you are looking for a comfortable pair of pants to hang around the house in or throw on to do errands, consider light athletic wear, like for example, yoga pants. Yoga pants are look enough to be comfortable and structured enough to look stylish. You can also throw on your favorite pair of jeans (find a pair with an elastic waist if buttoned styles aren't a good option for you) or clean, unripped sweatpants that fit properly.

It is possible to look good and be comfortable. You just have to find a style that works for you and stay away from the stirrups!

36| Invest In A Body Shaper

Body shapers are a good choice for just about any body type. Plus-sized women can benefit from the smooth, streamlined effect of a full-body shaper. It's important to note that your shaper should not be so tight that it leaves marks or makes you uncomfortable. The purpose isn't to suck you in too far, but to make your curves smooth under your clothing.

This is particularly poignant for dresses and outfits that hug your figure. Take advantage of stores that allow you to try on a body shaper before you purchase it. Sometimes, you need to purchase a shaper that is one size larger or smaller, depending on the manufacturer. Also, keep in mind that most body shapers have built in bras, so you should find a size that fits your bust as well.

37| Opt For Long Coat Instead Of A Bulky Sweater

During cold weather months, opt for a quarter-length coat in place of a bulky sweater. A long coat gives you a streamlined, polished effect and can work with day or evening wear, perfect for stylish plus-sizes.

Make sure the structure of the coat isn't too boxy, because that will only make you look wider than you really are. Look for a coat that drapes softly over your curves and gives you a nice, smooth silhouette. Don't go with too-big or too-small buttons that distract from the overall design of the coat — a good, quality coat wouldn't need that anyway!

Stay away from numerous embellishments and go with classic colors of white, navy or black. This will allow you to mix and match with other staples in your wardrobe.

38| Stay Away From "Painted-On" Jeans

Don't become victim to the muffin-top syndrome.

If your jeans are too tight and look "painted on," toss them and purchase a larger size. Jeans that are too tight and constricted only make plus-size women look bigger, and often cause the unsightly "muffin top syndrome." This unfortunate fashion faux-paus occurs when your jeans are too tight, causing your stomach to bulge over the top of the jeans. Not only is this uncomfortable, but it is a huge fashion don't! The best thing to remember is that all jeans look best when they fit properly. The perfect fit is within reach; it just takes a little searching to find the right pair.

39| Dresses For Plus-Size Figures

A fabulous dress can enhance the beautiful curves that accompany a plus-size figure. Empire waists, characterized by their high-waist design that falls just below the bust, are best for plus-sizes as they hide bulges and create a smooth contour.

The hemline should fall just above or below the knee for everyday styles; dressier gowns should fall above the ankles.

40| The Skinny On Swimsuits

There are a variety of swimsuits available for plus-sizes these days — and many of them have nothing to do with the bulky, full-coverage suits of the past. Plus-size swimwear is now getting just as fun and sexy as their smaller sized counterparts. Here is how the suits break down according to body type:

- If you are heavier on the bottom, go for a tankini with a skirted bottom. You want to go lighter in color on top and darker on the bottom for a balanced effect.

- If you are busty, go with a dark color and fuller cut on top and a light color on bottom. If you have great legs, show them off in a high-cut design.

- If you are trying to de-emphasize the stomach area, try a dark suit with embellishments around the bust area and a ruching detail around the tummy.

- If you are full-figured all over and fairly proportioned, go with a colorful one-piece with tummy and bust control.

Most experts recommend that you purchase a swimsuit a size larger than what you wear in regular clothing. However, it is important to try the suit on before you purchase it because different brands will likely give you a different fit. You might wear a size smaller from one designer and two sizes larger in another. Try it on before you invest to save yourself the headache later.

41| Write Down Your Measurements Before You Start Shopping

Shopping is a sport for most women — and plus-sizes are no exception. However, most of us have a certain amount of time set aside for finding the latest fashions, so it is important to do your homework before heading out the door. Start by writing down your measurements. This is especially important if you plan to shop online. You need bust, waist and hip sizes.

Try on some of your existing wardrobe to get a good idea of what your number size is (16, 18, 20, etc.) and your letter size is (XL, 1X, 2X, 3X, etc.). Also, write down special notes (things like wearing a specific size in a particular brand, etc.). Armed with this information, you are ready to shop.

→

42| Elongate Your Silhouette To Look Smoother

It's not about looking skinnier, it is about looking longer and smoother. Many plus-size women are happy with their curves and do not strive to dress "thinner." They simply want clothing that will flatter what they have. By creating an elongated silhouette, you look smoother and sleeker.

Pieces that help you to achieve this look include v-neck tops, high heels and outfits with a monochromatic theme. Avoid clothing that is too tight — this will not flatter your curves at all.

43| Best Plus-Size Denim Brands

Try on jeans before you purchase them. Take note of everything, from how they feel to how they fit around your waist, how long they are, how they flatter your midsection, backside and legs. Some of the best plus-size brands for jeans include:

- *Venezia*: Marketed through Lane Bryant, Venezia has long been a plus-size denim staple. Venezia jeans have optimal tummy control and a great overall slimming look. From dark denim to light wash, they look best dressed up. Perfect for a night out; try a rhinestone-studded belt and sexy, lacy cami with light wash, slightly flared Venezia jeans.

- *Seven7*: Finally, designer jeans for plus-sized women! Also marketed exclusively through Lane Bryant, plus-sized women everywhere celebrated when Seven7 jeans announced they were designing a version of their much-celebrated, designer denim for curvy types. Not to be confused with the *Seven for All Mankind* brand, Seven7 jeans have been popular with smaller sizes for quite some time. The full-figured version has a variety of washes that are figure flattering and easily transition from day to night.

- *Ashley Stewart*: Ashley Stewart's line of dark denim, bootcut jeans are a hands-down favorite because of their hip-slimming, booty-lifting qualities. They look good with a t-shirt and flats or a tailored jacket and matching cami. Ashley Stewart jeans are versatile and look great on all plus-size figures.

Baby Phat. Kimora Lee Simmons was also one of the first mainstream fashion designers to recognize the need for designer jeans for plus-sized women. Emblazoned with the classic, Baby Phat logo, these are the go-to jeans when you are looking for a shot of body confidence. They have great tummy control and have the best variety of colors and washes — from dark denim to elaborate embellishments. From conservative to wild, everyone can find their perfect pair of jeans in Baby Phat's plus size denim designs

Old Navy. Old Navy perfected the low-rise cut. These jeans sit low on your waist, avoiding stomach bulge. While dark denim usually looks best on plus-sizes, Old Navy's Rocker Flare Plus-Size Jeans in Authentic wash are both stylish and comfortable. They have a permanent crease, a whisker accent and look great with a funky, retro-striped top or rocker tee and chunky accessories.

44| T-Shirts: Finding The Perfect Style Every Time

Even t-shirts need careful consideration: too snug clothing emphasizes bulges; too loose makes you look bigger. Here are some things to keep in mind for your next t-shirt purchase:

- Avoid tees with busy designs (think large flowers or cartoon characters) – they are distracting and make you look like a walking advertisement!

- Baby tees do not generally look good on plus sizes. You want a nice, loose fit that falls right below the waist.

- Your tee should fit well around the neckline and sleeves as well as through your midsection. A too-tight tee can emphasize big arms, a thick neck and midriff bulges. To avoid this, remember the skimming philosophy: clothing should skim along your curves for a smooth contour.

- Stay away from tees that are excessively baggy! This makes you look bigger and sloppy.

- Solid colors are the most versatile; keep printed tees to a minimum

- Slogan tees are fun, but keep it clean and witty.

45| Sleepwear Secrets

Fun, new styles in sleepwear is one of the well-kept secrets of plus-size women's fashion. There are more options in sleepwear than there ever has been and now fuller figures can find a variety of PJs from sexy to comfortable and casual. To find the best type for you, keep these tips in mind:

- Don't be afraid to experiment with different styles and designs. Plus-size sleepwear comes in shorts or pants; flannel or silk; t-shirts or camis; sets or separates. Get creative and try prints, funky designs and soft fabrics.

- Make sure sexy is comfortable. Do not try to be so cute and sexy that you cannot get comfortable when you go to bed. Button-down pajamas with flannel bottoms, long, silk nightgowns and cami/shorts sets can be sexy and comfortable.

- Try to maintain breast support throughout the night. If you have a large bust, opt for a cami with built in bra support to hold you in place all night long.

- Throw away sleepwear that has run its course. Anything with holes, tears, stains, frays, etc. falls into this category.

46| Proper Fitting Undergarments Enhance Overall Outfit

Your outfit means nothing without the right undergarments. Proper-fitting undergarments are the key to getting your clothes to fit right. You should not wear anything that is uncomfortable or leaves angry, red marks on your skin.

- Underwear that is too tight with the elastic falling off should go in the garbage — immediately!

- Bras that leave marks in your skin or do not give your breasts proper support should be tossed as well! Get properly fitted for a good, sturdy bra that holds your breasts firmly in place. Straps should stay put and the band should be comfortable.

In addition, unless they are thongs, your panties should cover your behind, not bunch up in it. The right fit underneath your clothing will help you look better and feel more confident.

47| A Professional Wardrobe Begins At Home

When putting together a professional wardrobe, start at home. Clean out your closet: before you add to clothing, it is a good idea to take stock of what you already have.

You might be surprised to learn that you already own a few timeless pieces that are great for the workplace. Give pieces you no longer wear to charity or a friend.

With your closet under control, it is time to go shopping. Before you actually purchase new pieces, look around — both online and in your favorite boutiques. Check out large, name brand, plus-size retailers online if they are not located in your town.

Take stock of the latest trends and retailers that carry classic pieces. Remember, you are not looking for seasonal separates — you want to purchase clothing that will wear well several seasons from now. You are also looking for clothing that will wear well through a workday. Comfort is a big factor here.

48| Essential Professional Wardrobe Ideas

There are ten pieces you need to own to have the quintessential professional wardrobe. They include:

- The Perfect White Shirt
- Lightweight Knit Sweater
- All-Purpose Handbag
- Power Suit
- Everyday Jacket
- Sexy Flats
- Dark Trousers
- Red Accessories
- Pencil Skirt
- Closed-Toe Pumps

49| Dos And Don'ts Of Workplace Fashion

Your reputation at the office is important and let's face it — wearing the wrong thing can bring about bad word of mouth — which can unfortunately have an effect on your career regardless of your potential. Here are some dos and don'ts for the office so you can look — and perform — your best in your professional life.

DO dress to blend. If everyone in your office comes to work looking uber-professional, do not show up in slouchy jeans and a tank top. In turn, if your office is very laid-back, dress accordingly — meaning casual, but neat.

DON'T bring the club to work. Just about anything you would wear out for a night of clubbing is not a good idea for work — no matter how cute it is.

DO have confidence in yourself — professionally and personally. Your wardrobe is a reflection of how you feel about yourself. Work it accordingly!

DON'T be afraid to wear bold power suits or incorporate funky trends into your workplace fashions. You are full-figured and have the ability to be as fashionable as the next person has. Tell yourself that and learn to believe it!

50| Casual Officewear Dont's

When working in a office with a casual dress code policy, it's hard to know what kind of clothing is okay and what is just too-casual. If you get too laid-back with your wardrobe, you run the risk of being seen as a person who does not take their job seriously enough. Here are ten no-nos for office fashion, even in a casual environment:

- Sweatpants (of any kind, fabric or color)
- Jeans with holes, frays, patches or loud embellishments
- Long, baggy t-shirts
- Midriff-baring shirts
- Short shorts
- See-through or mesh anything
- Dirty, raggedy sneakers
- Miniskirts
- Extreme cleavage baring tops
- Tube tops (or any other strapless top) without a jacket

51| Work Attire Should Combine Comfort And Style

All too often, when we are caught up in trying to stay stylish, we negate the comfort factor of an outfit. This is especially true when it comes to footwear. Go for comfort.

You can be trendy, cute and comfortable by investing some time and effort to find three main pairs of shoes for work: amazing stilettos, mid-range pumps and a sexy pair of flats.

Reserve stilettos for those days when you need an extra dose of confidence – such as a presentation or a meeting with a new client. Only wear them if you plan to keep your movement to a minimum to avoid soreness at the end of the day.

The mid-rage pump should be your everyday shoe. A chunky heel is usually best as it offers your foot added support. Choose a neutral color that goes with most of the items in your professional wardrobe. If need be, add a gel insert into your shoe for extra comfort.

Save your flats for more casual days or trendy outfits. They will likely be more comfortable, so wear them on a day when you need to do a lot of walking or moving around the office.

52| The Trick To A Good Button-Down Fit

Button-down shirts are one of the staples of professional wardrobes. However, for fuller figures, they can be tricky to wear. It is important that your button-down top fit properly, otherwise you could end up with unsightly openings between buttons or an ill-fitting, clingy look.

The key to wearing a button-down shirt properly is to make sure it fits loosely enough to drape over your curves. It should be roomy in the bust area so the buttons do not strain.

Avoid tucking it into your pants unless it falls past your zipper area. A button-down shirt can make you look very professional, when worn correctly. Fit is everything — so be sure you try it on before purchase.

53| The Truth About Suits

Most women know that a good suit can make you feel — and look — like a million bucks. However, it is so important to consider the fit and style of a suit before you buy. Even the most expensive suit can look downright dowdy if it does not fit right.

For plus-sizes, avoid double-breasted suit jackets — they only make you look wider. Instead, opt for a single-breasted style for a smoother look. Go for longer-length jackets that give you a leaner look. Shorter, boxy styles tend to make plus-sizes look wider.

Skirts should fall over the contours of your body (without clinging) and look best when they hit right above the knee. If you find that your suit fits well in the waist, but droops everywhere else, get it tailored to fit your shape.

54| Accessorize Your Workwear

Accessories are super important when it comes to professional fashion for plus-sizes. Scarves, for example, are a great way to dress up a suit. Short scarves tied around the neck or longer scarves around collar and lapel of the jacket can add color or an interesting pattern to your suit.

Chunky gold or silver jewelry is also a great way to accessorize a work wardrobe. This kind of accessory looks chic and sophisticated. Stay away from too-trendy baubles, as they will make your outfit look less professional.

Handbags should also be professional. Stick with classic colors like black, grey, deep red or navy; they go with just about any outfit.

Choose a medium size handbag for the office. Too small and everything will burst out every time you go to get a pen; likewise, if your bag can hold an entire change of clothes, it is likely too large for work.

55| Don't Forget Your Blouse

When wearing a suit, beware of what's underneath.

The type of top you are wearing is important because it has an effect on how the suit looks overall, and will have to carry the outfit should you take your suit jacket off. Short-sleeved, silk or knit shells look great on full-figures and do not cling to your hotspots in an unflattering way. Long-sleeves are also a good option, but only in cooler weather. Your top should not be too tight or low cut; the style should fall within the overall parameters of your office dress code.

56| Bootcut Is Best

Bootcut trousers are the best cut for plus-sizes. When pants taper in at the ankle, they can have a disproportionate effect on your midsection, making it look fuller.

Instead, opt for the straight, sleek line of a bootcut. It is also important not to go too baggy with trousers; this will only make you look bigger.

Get pants tailored to fit properly to create a smooth contour. For plus-sizes with a thicker midsection, wear a thinner belt with trousers to avoid drawing attention to your midsection.

57| Belts Have Made A Comeback

Belts have come back in a big way. Plus-size designers are pairing belts worn high on the waist with long, button-down shirts (mostly solid colors such as white, black or red). Paired with denim jeans or a pair of black trousers, this look works well on plus-size shapes.

For a low-slung look, wear belts low on the waist. Rhinestone-studded and beaded belts are an attractive plus-size option for this look, best worn with sexy tops for night.

58| Proportion Is Important When It Comes To Jewelry

Proportion is everything when it comes to accessorizing for plus-sizes. Too big can be overpowering; too small can make you look even bigger. When it comes to jewelry including earrings, bracelets and rings, this rule doesn't always apply.

However, necklaces should vary in size depending on what you are wearing. If you are wearing a busy top, with a lot of prints or embellishments, go smaller and daintier around the neck area.

If you have a thick neck, stay away from chokers and small necklaces. Longer chains look good with low-cut tops and chunky, beaded jewelry can jazz up a plain outfit.

59| Footwear Facts

Many trendy shoe styles come in wider sizes to accommodate larger feet. So do not attempt to stuff your foot into an average size if you have wide feet. Not only will this cause extreme discomfort, but also can cause calluses and corns on your feet from ill-fitting shoes.

Wider sizes offer better support and more space for your foot. They will fit more comfortably as well. Likewise, do not assume that just because you have a full figure, you should wear a wide size.

Additionally, some footwear cannot be found in wider sizes because foot measurements are not the only consideration. Knee-high boots, for example, are not usually found in wide sizes because the thickness of the calf is an additional factor in the overall fit. To combat this problem, look for materials that stretch to fit your foot and calf.

Before investing in shoes or boots of any kind, get your foot measured properly. This is the only way to ensure that you get a perfect shoe fit.

60| Hats On For A New Look

To really spice up an outfit, don a fun, colorful hat. Hats are a great way to add personality to your outfit — and cover up a bad hair day. It is important to tailor your hat to fit the occasion.

For example, you do not want to wear your favorite worn-in college baseball cap to the office. Purchase hats with your existing wardrobe in mind. Each hat should have an outfit; otherwise, you will never wear it.

Baseball caps should be reserved for days spend running errands or going to the park. Fedoras and newsboy caps are great for nights on the town. Small, colorful straw hats are good the office (though they might not last the entire day because of the comfort factor).

Wide-brim, natural straw hats are great for just about any occasion. Do not always try to hide your hair under a hat; sometimes, it is a good idea to style around your hat in case you have to remove it.

61| Pay Attention To Handbag Size And Color

The size of your handbag matters more than you think. Large handbags work well for plus-sizes because they proportion your overall shape.

Small handbags are okay for special occasions, but not for every day. Not only are they too small to hold everything you need, but they make you look bigger because of their small size.

It also pays to keep the color and pattern on your bag neutral enough to wear with anything. Funky colors and bags with big logos are okay to use when you are out on the weekends or in the evenings. For the office, keep it professional with blacks or grays.

62| Opt For Fine Jewelry

For extra-special occasions, skip the cocktail jewelry and go with the real thing. Fine jewelry can add class to an outfit; whereas cocktail jewelry can downplay the look you are trying to achieve.

Fine jewelry does not have to be expensive; instead focus on less-expensive jewels that are quality-made.

Stones should have the right style and cut; they should fit in their settings accordingly. Consult with a jeweler on what you are looking for, what your outfit looks like and what kind of style suits you.

63| Accessories Know No Limit

There is no limit to the accessories available to fuller figured women. This is one area where your overall size does not matter. Find styles that work with your clothing personality and, with the exception of handbags, do not choose according to size considerations. Experiment with jewelry and other accessories and wear what looks good on you.

64| Watches Are All-Purpose Accessory

Not only are watches a great way to keep track of time, they are also a great fashion statement. It is important to keep an everyday style as your core timepiece.

However, have fun with your watches on weekends and special occasions. Change it up from night to day. Wear a necklace timepiece. Check out one of those watches that double as a bracelet.

These days, watches come in elaborate colors and styles; change them as much as you change your outfit. So let loose and have fun with new trends.

→

65| The Facts About Hosiery And Plus-Sizes

Hosiery and plus-size women have a love-hate relationship. There is nothing worse than trying to squeeze into a too-tight pair of pantyhose just to have them run once you have finally struggled into them. In the past, there were limited options for plus-size women, but the hosiery industry has come a long way since that point.

There are now several brands of hosiery geared towards plus-size women that make it easy to slide a pair of pantyhose without the assistance of the fire department. Control tops are helpful to help smooth out your curves, however, do not sacrifice comfort for style. Pantyhose should fit comfortably and allow relative ease of movement. Keep these tips in mind:

- If you cannot squat down in them, they are not the right size!

- If they roll down, they are not the right size!

- If the area that fits around your crotch is down around your thighs, they are not the right size.

Do not get so hung on the number of the size you are wearing, that you are not willing to go up a size or two to get the right fit.

66| Limit Hair Accessories

Beware of hair accessories — ones that are too bright or complex can look unprofessional. Hair accessories that wear well for the office and beyond include dark-colored pins, tortoise-shell hair clips, neutral colored headbands and hair clips that hold updos in place.

Scarves are always a great choice in hair accessories; just stay away from busy patterns. Choose accessories that complement your outfit — not draw attention away from it.

67| Sports Bra Is Most Important Element Of Plus-Size Workout Wardrobe

A proper-fitting sports bra is the most important element of a plus-size woman's fitness wardrobe. A sports bra helps to give you the proper support to hold your breasts in place while you work out. This is especially important for women with a large bust.

Finding the right sports bra starts with knowing your measurements. Don't buy a sports bra based on the size you think you are; take the time to actually go and get measured for the right specifications. Then, choose several different brands and try them on before you purchase anything. Different brands have different amenities and it's important to know which ones work for your body type.

The most common feature found from brand to brand is moisture-wicking, which will help to keep you cool and dry throughout your workout. Wide straps will help keep your breasts lifted and supported, without the discomfort sometimes caused by smaller straps. Most sports bras come in a soft cup design, which helps to make you more comfortable during your workout.

68| Make Your Workout Wardrobe Stylish

If you're going to take the time to go to the gym, sweat off those extra calories and subsequently ache the next morning from sore muscles, you might as well look good while doing it! Forget the ripped sweatpants and stained t-shirts. When you are putting together a workout wardrobe, stay stylish. Not only will you look good, but you'll feel good.

A stylish workout wardrobe can motivate you to get outside or walk a few extra miles on the treadmill. Think of it like you do a new outfit: anytime you get a new shirt or skirt, you can't wait to go somewhere so you can wear it. Stylish exercise clothing gives you a little extra push to work out even when you would rather be on the sofa watching old movies.

Find bright reds, blues and yellows — colors that will help you pep up! Purchase pants with designs and accessories to match your outfits.

Get comfortable styles that still flatter your body type. The most basic rule of fashion applies here — if you look good, you will gain the confidence to want to show off your style — even when working out!

69| Stay Away From Spandex

Stay away from spandex. It is simply not that generous to curvy body types, outside of the undergarment arena. Clothing with spandex are often touted for their slimming effects, which is fine in small amounts. However, it's not worth it to look slimmer and suffer through an entire aerobics class in a pair of too-tight spandex shorts!

Opt for clothing that fits loosely over the curves of your body. It's important that your clothing move with you when engaging in sports. This will increase your overall efficiency.

Comfort is also a huge factor. If you aren't comfortable, you aren't going to perform well. Look for airy cotton fabrics and stay away from anything that feels tight or restrictive.

Top athletic clothing brands are usually the most reliable, however, retail stores don't always carry larger sizes in stock. If you don't see your size, go online or call the manufacturer directly to see if they have merchandise in your size and how you can purchase it.

70| Find Proper Footwear

Always, always, always wear the proper footwear. This is particularly poignant for plus-sizes, because the right support on your feet can determine how your lower body will react to exercise or sports activities.

Many major brands make choosing the right footwear easy for you because athletic shoes are marketed by activity. For example, Nike remains the premier choice for runners. Reebok makes a Sweet Surf Mesh model that is great for aerobics activity. The Adidas Lyte Speed GCS shoe is perfect for basketball players as it has been designed for quick directional changes.

Many plus-size women look for shoes in wide widths. Similar to clothing, retailers might not carry wide widths, but the manufacturer could make those large, wider styles. It's worth your time to go online or call to find out. It's important to your exercise or sports regimen to have the right support on your feet!

71| Look For Athletic Wear According To Activity

Think light when it comes to workout clothing. Heavy, bulky fabrics make you look bigger and feel heavier. Super-light cottons that fit loosely are perfect for transitioning between various activities. The key to finding great plus-size athletic wear is to search for pieces that perform according to activity. For example, Old Navy makes a Yoga Pant that fits over curvy bodies and is supremely comfortable. These pants are great for running, walking, aerobics and more! Lane Bryant makes a mesh-inset short that touts ease of movement, which is perfect for runners or brisk walkers. Avenue's Casual Cotton Hooded Tee make biking — indoors or out — cozy and comfy.

72| Accessorize Your Workout Style

Accessories are not only important to everyday style, but also to workout clothing. Look for special holders for your water and/or iPod. Many of these holders are quite fashionable and can be found in a variety of designs, colors and styles.

Having both of these things readily available during your workout or activity decreases the need to stop in the middle of your session.

Also, look for fun and funky ponytail holders for your hair and matching sweatbands for your head and arms. Fingerless gloves provide protection for your hands during weightlifting and give you a retro edge to your style.

73| Make Exercise Fun

Plus-size women are becoming more and more active, sparking a huge revolution among fuller figures to focus on being active and healthy, instead of numbers on a scale.

From biking to training for marathons, plus-size women are finding that they can join in on many of the activities their smaller counterparts are doing.

For example, if you are looking for a fun activity, try spinning or Pilates. Don't let your weight or size intimidate you — and definitely don't compare yourself to the other people in class around you. You are fabulous and trying to get healthy just like everyone else and finding an activity that is fun and keeps your interest will help you in that endeavor.

74| Change Clothing Every Two Days

When purchasing separates for a workout wardrobe, be sure to stock up. Though they may live in your gym bag for days at a time, it's generally not a good idea to wear the same clothing for several days in a row. Most of the time, you sweat in your workout clothes, making them wet and....well....smelly!

Change it up daily. Be careful not to let workout gear hang out in your gym bag, it will only get stinkier and cause everything else in the bag to smell like a sweaty workout!

75| Layer For Plus-Size Athletic Fashion

Layering makes for fantastic athletic fashion. It works well for plus-sizes because it allows you to wear trendy workout pieces, while still maintaining coverage over your curvy figure.

You might try experimenting with belly-baring tops and high-waisted workout pants under a baggy, airy tank. Or you can do a form-fitting tee with yoga pants. You might try wearing a colorful sports bra and a thin, white top and matching running pants. Choose outfits according to your body type and layer accordingly.

Of course, it's important to note that you don't want to layer too much because as you work out and sweat, you should be able to shed some of your pieces, if necessary.

76| Wear Socks When Working Out

Don't forget your socks. Working out without socks, particularly when wearing sneakers, can help contribute to foot fungus and other conditions and infections. This happens because of the amount of chafing, movement and sweating that happens around your feet as you exercise.

If you find socks to be uncomfortable, try a thin, ankle style sock that has a barely-there feel, but still provides a protective layer between your shoe and your foot. Because let's face it, in addition to the infection and chafing factors, you simply don't want to mess up your gorgeous pedicure working out without socks!

77| Baggy Is Not Better

Perhaps the most important rule of plus-size fashion for teens has nothing to do with seasons, wardrobe staples or any of the other usual style terms. The right fit is everything in plus-size teen fashion.

All too often, teens make the common mistake of dressing in baggy clothing to hide a plus-size figure. Unfortunately, this only makes you look bigger. It is important for plus-size teenagers to come to terms with their shape in order to dress in clothing that is flattering and makes them look better — not bigger.

Clothing should skim along the curves of your body. Too clingy? Toss it! Too baggy? In the trash. Look for the fit that is just right!

78| Avoid Low-Rise Jeans

Low-rise jeans are a plus-size teen's enemy! This style of jean often causes unsightly bulges in all the wrong places — think "muffin top" and weird hip bulge. Instead, look for at waist jeans that sit right at your waist. The right fit it also important. To keep a trendy look, buy bootcut, dark wash jeans. Dark denim looks great on plus-sizes and wears well with just about anything.

79| Layering Allows Plus-Sizes To Work Within Trends

Layering is one of the best components of plus-size teen fashion. First, it is already trendy among most sizes, so you fit right in.

Second, layering allows you to wear things you might not otherwise look good wearing. For example, midriff baring tops do not always translate to plus-sizes.

However, layered over another longer, thinner shirt makes the top look great! The same applies to cropped sweaters. A huge plus-size trend is layering a cropped sweater over a longer, button-down top.

Again, by layering clothing, you can cultivate a creative, fabulous look. Try to layer with thinner fabrics so you do not end up looking bigger and bulkier than you really are. It is possible to make trendy pieces work for you; it just takes a little ingenuity on your part to make it work for your size.

80| Keep Fashion In Tune With Your Body Type

Take your time when shopping fashions for plus-size teens. Find styles that complement your shape instead of trying to wear the latest fads.

Your sense of style is in place to express your individuality, a fact that most teens have a hard time dealing with. However, for plus-size teens, it is extra important not to be sucked into trying to look like everyone else.

Instead, try to focus on core styles that work for you and flatter your curves. Save blending in for your shoes, accessories and a few trendy pieces that do translate well to your size.

81| Buy Clothing For The Size Your Are Now

Don't purchase clothing for the size you want to be. Buying clothes in a size smaller than what you wear in anticipation of losing weight will simply not fit properly — which means they will not look good — and you will only set yourself up for disappointment. Do not buy clothing in the hopes that you will change your overall shape. Buy for the size and shape you are now.

If you lose weight, you can always buy new clothes or have your old ones altered.

Instead, focus on being healthy and embrace your curves and the clothing that makes them look good.

82| Make A Flipbook Of Your Favorite Trends

Make a file of your favorite looks. This helps you to be clear when you hit the mall for some new clothes. As you flip through magazines, cut out pictures of trends you think might work well for your figure. If you look online, print out photos of pieces you like. Then, when you go shopping, take your file with you and match up what is in your file with what is in stores. It might sound like a lot of work, but if you want to be stylish and look good – it pays to put in some extra effort. There are so many different trends and ideas hitting you when you are actually in the store, it is easy to lose focus from the look you are trying to achieve. A little flipbook of your favorite styles can help you to be clear.

83| Skinny Jeans Can Work On Plus-Sizes

Skinny jeans have made a huge comeback and are everywhere from fashion mags to celebrities. But don't let the word "skinny" fool you - this trend translates well to plus-sizes, particularly if you have great legs. The trick is to wear a long, colorful tunic-style top if you have a thicker midsection. Avoid looking bigger than you really are by choosing the right size tunic; too roomy can work against you. Instead, look for a tunic that flares out just slightly at the waist and stops about mid-thigh. If your legs are thick, wear knee-high boots to add balance to your outfit.

Keep in mind that this trend is not to be confused with a tapered leg look. Skinny legs should still have the straight, smooth silhouette that works well for fuller figures.

84| Cinched Jackets Create Midsection

Cinched jackets are a great look for plus-sized teens. They create a waist — even if you do not really have one — and help to minimize the stomach area.

You can also get this effect by adding a belt to a regular, button-down jacket. There are varieties of different looks that work well with a cinched jacket.

For example, a pair of dark, bootcut jeans and a solid-colored button-down top with a cinched jacket looks fabulously trendy. Make sure the top is longer than the jacket to attain an overall slimming effect.

85| Tips For Online Purchases

Shopping online for great plus-size clothing can be convenient, quick and easy. It not only saves you time, but oftentimes you can find great deals. However, when buying online, here are a few things to keep in mind:

- Know your measurements. This is important because you do not have the benefit of a dressing room when shopping online. You have to be able to peg your exact size, so knowing all of your measurements can help you make the right choice.

- Pay attention to fabrics – they are just as important as size. A silk or and chiffon won't have the same "give" that a cotton or stretch fabric will, so pay attention to those details before making a purchase. If you fit just right into a size 18/20, consider going a half-size or full-size larger if the fabric is restrictive. Be aware of how your body generally looks in these fabrics and purchase accordingly.

86| Bohemian Chic On Curvy Figures

A trend that works well for plus-size teens is the bohemian chic look. Teens wear this look because of the individuality it reflects and the way it transcends different cultures and styles. The key to getting the boho chic look right is to make it look like you put forth little to no effort at all.

To put together a great boho wardrobe, you need these key pieces:

- A beaded tank (preferably in a neutral color like tan, brown, white or black)

- Funky, wooden jewelry

- A stunning peasant skirt (this is the place to infuse some color — try turquoise, red or deep gold)

- Flared jeans

- Long, beaded necklaces

- Chunky turquoise jewelry

- A cropped, button-down top to layer over your tank

All of these pieces look great on curvier figures. Remember, however, not to overdo it on one outfit. Instead, pair a peasant skirt with a plain tank and funky jewelry. On the other hand, try a bright, flowing tunic with embellished jeans and beaded flip-flops. The idea is to look relaxed and natural.

87| Clip Plus-Size Looks

Clip your favorite plus-size looks from various magazines and Web sites. Then, start looking at your local sales circulars. Flip through them and check out trendy, plus-size items that are on sale.

Clip out the coupons and save the circulars in your purse, so you have them with you when you begin shopping. Compare what you have with your plus-size clippings to see how you can translate the look for less while you are going from store to store.

88| Tips For Getting Great (And Sometimes Hidden) Deals

During your shopping trip, remember that many stores have a policy of offering customers the sale price for an item the day before and day after the sales begins and ends. In most instances, you just have to ask!

When you are ready to hit the stores, shop the clearance section first. This is a handy tip for in-store or online purchases. By checking out the clearance section in the store or on a Web site, you can save up to 75% on some items. Clearance racks are usually found in the back of the store or at the bottom of the store's home page. It's worth searching for — you'll be shocked by the money you can save.

89| Purchase Wardrobe Staples Off-Season

Maybe you're not a shopaholic, or even a savvy shopper. If you aren't one to indulge in the latest plus-size fashion trends, purchase wardrobe staples that are off-season. You can get a fabulous bathing suit for next to nothing if you purchase it during the fall or winter. The same rule applies for winter clothes — buy them during the summer and save a bunch of money!

Make sure you are constantly taking note of what plus-size staples you currently have in your closet and what you need. Look over each article of clothing to make sure it's still in good shape and toss what must be replaced. Keep a running list so you can get what you need when you come across a great deal!

90| How Important Is It To Find A Good Deal?

We're all constantly looking for a good deal. In the end, finding an exact item for a bargain price could be a waiting game. Depending on how trendy the item, how much you want it and how expensive the item is will determine whether it's a good idea to wait for it to go on sale. Translating plus-size style on a budget can be difficult, so consider carefully how important the item is to you, and your wardrobe!

91| Get Online For Great Deals

When you get home, make a list of the items you wanted, but weren't able to find at a bargain price. Now, it is time to get online. The first place to go is the clearance or sale tab. Peruse through this area to see what kind of deal you get. Often, you can score some great finds in the online clearance/sale section, especially with plus-size retailers that only operate online.

Make a list of your specific measurements and how fabrics generally drape over your curves. Cross-reference with it before you make a purchase. This will enable you to make informed choices when purchasing clearance items, which are often nonrefundable.

92| Lighten Up

All too often, plus-sized women are stuck in the trap of wearing dark colored clothing. It's true, darker clothing does has a slimming effect on a fuller figure, which is the origin of this fashion principle. However, it is important that your clothing reflect your personality, as well as flatter your shape. Plus-sized women can look good in all colors, so let loose and have fun with your wardrobe.

Mix and match bright colors with solid separates for a vivacious, fun-loving look. Try tops in bright, bold reds or cool turquoise colors and capri pants in hot pink or coral. Get bold and wear a dress in a tropical hue of lemon or orange.

The key to wearing color is to wear it on your best body part. For example, if you have great legs, show them off in a flirty, colorful skirt and wear a darker color on top. Make sure the skirt is the focal point of the outfit.

Keep in mind that bright colors are often in style according to season so your outfits should fluctuate accordingly. For fall and winter months, choose rich, deep colors, like dark red, navy, orange, deep purple, chocolate and, of course, black. When spring and summer hits, lighten up your wardrobe with pinks, yellows, light blues, white, lilac, coral and light browns and tans.

Whatever you choose, jazz up your style with color and show the world your great personality through fashion!

93| Wrap Yourself In A Wrap Shirt

Wrap shirts are a plus-sized gal's best friend! A wrap shirt hugs your curves in just the right way, making you look streamlined and smooth. Wrap shirts can go with any outfit and designers always find ways to work them into the latest trends.

Choose solid colors instead of busy prints to make the shirt's versatility work for your wardrobe. Wrap shirts come in a variety of styles from a classic wrap to a faux-wrap look on the front and really enhance the beauty of a curvy figure.

94| Exude Professionalism In a Power Suit

A power suit should be a wardrobe staple because with the right shirt, it is versatile enough to go from work to play. Pair up a power suit with a three-quarter length jacket and pants that hit the just below the ankle with a classic pair of chunky heels for a professional, plus-sized trend that never goes out of style.

This look works best when pants and jackets are the same shade. The monochromatic tone of the colors gives off a slimming effect; save the prints the shirt or camisole you wear underneath the suit. Funky accessories are the best way to make a statement with this look.

Fabric is an important consideration as well. Generally, suits in heavier fabrics, such as tweed or wool, should be reserved for the cooler months. Wear lighter, airier cottons and linens during spring and summer.

95| Knee-Length Shorts Are Here To Stay

Knee-length shorts stormed the plus-sized fashion market in early 2006 and have yet to show signs of fading in popularity. This style is a great option for plus-sized women who traditionally shy away from wearing shorts. Knee-length shorts look best when they hit just above the knee. Some styles are cuffed; some are not — this is a personal style preference, as either way looks good.

For the office, wear them with a collared, button-down shirt and high heels. For play, throw on your favorite tank and a pair of casual flats. To dress them up, try a form-fitting top with a funky belt and bold accessories.

96| Tunics, Tunics Everywhere

Tunics are a plus-size fashion "do" and are versatile enough to work for any occasion. Tunics skim along the curves of your figure to show off your shapeliness, but not so tightly that any bumps and bulges show. Flowing, colorful tunics are great for plus-sizes because they fit loosely and comfortably, often coming in closer at the top and flaring out slightly towards the waist, similar to empire styles.

Going out? Pair a silk or chiffon, v-neck, Asian-print tunic with a pair of dark-colored, knee-length shorts, solid-colored high-heels and bright, dazzling accessories.

Picnic time? Try a lightweight, cotton tunic with denim capris and a funky pair of round-toe flats. For added style, throw on a newsboy cap and accessorize with silver jewelry.

For the office? Exude confidence in knit, striped or patterned tunics (black and red are a great combo!) with black slacks and reptilian pumps (think croc!). Jewelry can be bold — a retro red and black mix — or muted — skinny gold or silver jewelry — depending on your personal preference

→

97| Corsets Made A Comeback — And Are Here To Stay

One of the coolest trends to hit the plus-size fashion industry is the corset. Corsets made a vintage comeback at the millennium and have managed to stay around. Hot retailers, like Ashley Stewart and Avenue, are still managing to incorporate them into their seasonal lines, with funky new ideas.

Corsets cinch the waist in slightly (without being uncomfortable), giving you a nice, slight hourglass figure (even if you are not naturally shaped that way). The best part is that this look can go for day or night.

For the office, stick with a black or white corset and pair it with black trousers and a long white shirt. If you want to jazz up your outfit, add color with your choice of accessories. Red would be an obvious option here, but you can also wear blue, green or purple for something different. If you are a little more daring, go with yellow, lizard print heels or blue patent leather, peep-toe platform heels with multi-colored accessories on top.

For night, open the buttons on the shirt and go with another color corest like a metallic gold or silver. Sequined or glittery shoes would be a great option with this outfit.

The key to wearing a corset is to wear it with confidence. It is perhaps one of the best pieces to show off your curves in a flattering light.

98| Beware of Ruffles

While it is considered one of the more romantic looks, ruffled shirts should be worn with care. They often add an unnecessary (and unflattering) layer to tops, which without any real structure, make a plus-size woman look bigger.

The key to ruffles is proportion. For plus-sizes, ruffles look best on sleeves. If you are going to wear ruffles around the neckline, stick to one ruffle and make sure it's not too big. A ruffle that is too big looks unflattering to your bust; too small and it makes the rest of you look even bigger. To be on the safe side, minimize ruffles and relegate them to shirt sleeves.

→

99| The Truth About Stripes

We've all heard the theory on stripes: horizontal stripes add depth to your figure and vertical stripes make you look slimmer. Now, let me break through the myth and dictate the fact about stripes.

Stripes are indeed tricky and require a little fashion ingenuity, but stripes, both horizontal and vertical, can look great of fuller figures. The trick to stripes lie in their size.

Plus-sizes look good wearing thin horizontal stripes. Save thicker stripes for vertical designs. The old adage is true that thick, horizontal stripes do make a full figure look wider. However, if the lines are small and thin, that effect is diminished greatly.

If possible, save horizontal stripes for suits and outfits with accompanying jackets. The layer over the shirt stops the eye — eliminating any "widening" effect.

Vertical and diagonal stripes can be bigger — but even here, do not go too big. Go with small to medium stripes and try to infuse color into the outfit to avoid a drab, lifeless look.

100| Skirts Can Make — Or Break — Your Overall Look

Skirts can really flatter a plus-sized shape. From a funky denim skirt to a feminine, flirty full-length floral, the variety of skirt styles for plus-sizes are endless. There are, however, a few skirt tips to keep in mind:

- Repeat after me: No pleats….ever. Pleats rarely look flattering on full figures. They make you look wider and in most cases have no style value for the plus-size woman.

- Pencil skirts are a wonderful addition to the market and look good on all full figures. They are narrow from the hips to right above or below your knee. They have a slimming quality, but make your best lower body curves really stand out. As an added bonus: all legs look great in the right pencil skirt!

- Long length flared skirts are another plus-sized "don't." They make you look bigger and they break up the lines of your outfit that make you look streamlined and smooth with an unsightly flare at the bottom.

101| Black Is Back, And Better Than Ever

Black is back! (Ok, it never really went away). In addition to the slimming effect it has on just about any type of figure, black also provides a polished, sophisticated and stylish look. From the little black dress (which no woman should be without) to a black power suit, black is back in a big way!

But heed this black beware: do not overdo it! Too much black can make you look austere and/or unapproachable. It is important to personalize your look when wearing black. For example, wear a crisp, classic white button-down shirt with a bold-hued accessory, such as cherry red, to complement a black suit. If you want to amp up the little black dress, choose large, sparkling jewels, such as diamonds or gemstones. Basic black pants can be work with a bright shirt, matching scarf and gold or silver accessories. Handbags are also a great way to infuse color into a black outfit.

Black is a plus-sized trend that never goes out of style. It has been — and always will be — the perfect go-to color when you are not sure what to wear or need a good dose of clothing confidence.

More Titles in the LifeTips Book Series

101 VACATION RENTAL TIPS
by Lynne Christen

101 AUTISM TIPS
by Tammi Reynolds

101 SPORTS APPAREL TIPS
by Heidi Splete

101 HEALTH INSURANCE TIPS
by Michelle Katz